Wealth, Women & War

By

Larry A. Yff

CHAPTERS

INTRODUCTION

History tells us King David loved war to an almost maniacal degree. His son, King Solomon, was more into wealth and women. They both were authors.

King David wrote a book called Psalm. It is pretty much full of praise songs about God, letters asking God to continue to help him win wars and "Dear Diary" letters to God whenever shit wasn't going to swell.

His son, King Solomon, wrote three books. They are Proverbs, Song of Songs and a book called Ecclesiastes. His books are lessons about money, sex, women and booze. I don't talk about Song of Songs in this book because honestly, to me it may have been beautiful in those days, but the shit was bizarre, confusing and creative with a sprinkle of crazy on top.

Their books were written thousands of years ago, but successful people still use them today. I love the beauty and the lessons in their books, but I don't understand what the fuck they are saying sometimes with all the "thou" and "thy" and "doth sayeth". If you have the same problem with some of the language in the Bible, this book is for you.

It's not like I just rewrote their songs and lessons and changed phrases like, "I doth want to gaze mine eyes upon thy lovely bosom" and changed it to, "Damn, girl! Let me see your titties!"

Well, I kind of did…it's hard to explain. Instead of me trying to tell you about it, just go ahead and start "to cast thine view upon such words as thou hast never seen with thine own eyes before."

What I'm saying to you in my words is to just start reading the book. Enjoy…

CHAPTER ONE

Psalm

King David wrote the book in the Bible called "Psalm." It has more than 100 chapters full of insight into his personal walk with God that will benefit Believers and non-Believers alike. A lot of them have the same, basic structure and template, but that's for good reason.

He was a warrior and loved war. Sometimes you win and sometimes you lose. When he was on a hot streak, his psalms reflect his emotions with lyrics of love for God and how God will and has never let him down. When his luck was cold as ice, his psalms reflected his emotions as well and were full of some of the darkest, gloomiest shit I ever read in my life.

And that's what makes his book a masterpiece. He is an example for us on how life can be with God, or at least how his walk with God was. He felt scared sometimes…and told us. He was super happy sometimes…and told us. He was kind of mad at God sometimes…and told us. I can relate to the ups and downs in life from a Believers standpoint and appreciate it. Whatever your walk in life is, worst-case scenario, there are some general lessons that could be learned from this warrior-king.

Let's take a look at some of them…

1. **Psalm 1:** As long as you stay away from people who aren't trying to do shit in life, you will be okay; especially if you enjoy studying God's laws. Just make sure you study the Bible every day and you will be successful in life.

2. **Psalm 2:** David is basically giving a warning to any king who tries to attack him. He's telling them to back the fuck up because he walks with God and there's no way they will be able to beat him…so they might as well stop trying. He also adds that their best bet is to make peace with him or they asses is grasses and God is the lawnmower. He

was always bold and made it known that the source of his boldness is God's presence and Spirit with him.

3. **Psalm 3:** He starts off on a very personal note that is full of emotion. He is going through something with one of his sons: his son is challenging his dad's throne. "Dear Diary, I have had to leave my Palace and go on the run because my son is trying to kill me and take over my throne." He ends it by giving himself a pep-talk by telling God, "I'm just going to relax, ok? I know you will make sure everything will be alright." He was never ashamed to come to God and let Him know he's a little scared or a lot scared, but His reassurance is knowing God will take care of him in a dark time like this family crisis.

4. **Psalm 4:** It appears as though some shit is not going too good in his kingdom. People are starting to ask questions and test his authority. He tells God, "I'm so done with this season and I'm looking forward to the good and prosperous times the people will enjoy again under my

rule." David often reassured himself by talking to himself.

Here he's letting God know, once again, that he knows

God will keep him safe. We also get to see a loving king

side of David, because he tells God that he will be happy

when the citizens under his rule are happy. It's as though

he gets depressed and feels bad when people are saying

mean things about him in times of trouble.

5. **Psalms 5, 6 and 7:** He is reminding God that he prays to

Him first thing in the morning and that he pays attention

to everything God tells him to do. I'm thinking there are a

lot of people around him being sneaky and telling lies on

him. It also sounds like his throne is under constant

attack and he is telling God, "Look, God, *I'm* the one who

trusts you and doesn't do a lot of wicked stuff...but *they*

do! You can go ahead and get mad and crush them for

messing with me, your faithful son, at any time now.

Thanks in advance." David had no problem talking to God

like we would talk to a security guard if somebody was

walking through a store wearing a long, black trench-coat, flashing his private parts to people: "Hey! Anytime now Mr. Security Guard, you can rush this guy, tackle him to the ground and handcuff him! What are you waiting for? The *real* police?!"

6. **Psalm 8:** He says something interesting here. He tells God that, "...through the praise of children and infants you have established a stronghold against evil..." He is letting us in on how the power of praise works and that even children and infants have the ability to give God the permission to attack His earthly enemies and wickedness on Earth. My wife and I have studied how trading in the spirit realm works and it was interesting to see David touch on that. Basically, it's the process Jesus talked about when He said, "Whatever you legally bind on Earth will be legally bound in Heaven." That means, when you ask Jesus for something with the faith and understanding that He can and will get us what we have asked for, that

legally binds who and whatever we need on Earth and in Heaven to answer our petition. Knowing the praise of a little child has that same affect is good to know. He also asks God, "What is it about us humans that You like so much? You have made us a little less than humans but have put us in charge of everything you have made…"

7. **Psalm 10**: Here David gets into a little bit of a challenge to God without challenging God. There must be a lot of wickedness and Wild West outlaw type shit going on because David seems like he's at his wits end, absolutely frustrated and can't seem to figure out why God isn't doing anything? He directly asks God why is He hiding during a time like this where robbers, thieves and murderers are having their way in the kingdom. The challenge part of this Psalm is when he says to God, "These wicked people who are having their way don't acknowledge you, they don't respect you and they act like they're not scared of you. Why aren't you doing anything

about that? What is it about this time and day that makes you just sit back and allow mere mortals to tear shit up and break damn near every law you've ever written without getting punished by You?" He ends this Psalm politely by saying, "I know you see what's happening and I know you hear the cry of those in need and I also know that in the end, I have no doubt that You will take care of business like you always do."

8. **Psalm 18:** This Psalm was written during the beginning of his reign as King of Judah. This is one of those really personal, heart-felt, personal thank-you to God. David was a man of war and a lot of his Psalms are war-related. Either they are giving God thanks and the credit for winning wars or he was asking God when was He going to kill his enemies for him. The beginning starts off with him talking about how much attack he was under and that just when it seemed like he was about to die and be overtaken, God reached down and rescued him. He says

God was mad that somebody had messed with His faithful

son David. Not just any kind of mad. David says God got

so mad smoke came out of His nostrils and He shot

arrows at David's enemies that were like flashes of

lightning. He then has a section where He explains why

God protects him. He credits it to being faithful to God

and following all the laws God has established. That is a

reoccurring theme and it started in the very first Psalm he

wrote. He follows this section up with one about how

God has given him the physical ability to wage war. This is

where you can feel his excitement with war! He's talking

about how his enemies were begging for mercy but he

didn't give a shit and crushed their skulls. He says that

some of them cried out to God to save them, but since

David is more blessed in God's eyes and has more favor

with God, God ignored their pleas and helped David kill all

of his enemies until none of them were left standing. The

last section is a summary. He sums up the fact of God

rescuing him, giving him ability to wage war, helped him use that ability to kill all the competition and then another "thank you" to God for making all the nations bow down and serve him, the king who God loves.

9. **Psalm 20:** David shifts his focus from himself to everybody out there who loves God. It's a prayer asking God to bless everyone who loves Him and give Him sacrifices. He asks God to give everyone who loves Him whatever it is they want and make all their plans successful and ends it by asking God to please answer them whenever they call on Him. David was big on sacrifices and following God's laws. He credits these actions with the reason why God continually gave him success and this Psalm lets us know that David sincerely wants everybody to feel the joy and security in God he has been feeling. One quick side note here: our modern-day sacrifice is completely different than the sacrifices in his day. During his day, sacrifices were made to God to

cover any current sins or to cover the sins for the past

year. That's the Old Testament covenant God made with

the people of that day. The New Testament covenant is

different. Jesus died and fulfilled the legal requirement of

a pure, human sacrifice and that eliminated the need for

all the cattle, sheep and other animal sacrifices of David's

day. The principle remains the same: honor and respect

the sacrifices that were made to keep us in right standing

with God.

10. **Psalm 22:** This Psalm is full of animal references and it

makes sense for a couple of reasons. One is that David

had fought lions and bears as a young man while he was

protecting his family's sheep and when warriors talk, they

tend to use animal references like, "I'm a beast." There

are also animal references used by and about Jesus. He is

described as being the Lamb of God, the Lion of Judah and

other animal terms. One time, when Jesus was irritated

with a lady who kept asking Him questions, He referred to

her and her culture as being a bunch of dogs. David talks

about how he was surrounded by powerful enemies he

called bulls and God saved him. He also talks about how

thieves are all around him like a pack of dogs. He says he

has to worry about the horns of oxen being ran through

him. He says warriors like lions are on the prowl against

him. But there is another reason: he feels like the lowest

form of shit and scum on the face of the Earth. He even

goes so far as to say he feels like he is less than human

and calls himself a worm. I wondered why he was feeling

like this with all the animal terms because I haven't read a

Psalm like this one before. I read a line where he talked

about people throwing stones at him like he was a piece

of shit and that he felt like everybody hated him. That's

when it hit me: while his son had chased him out of his

kingdom, David was on the run, walking with his Royal

caravan and somebody cursed him and threw rocks at

him. He describes this as one of the very lowest periods

in his life.

11. Psalm 23: This has to be the most famous of all David's

Psalms. What is it that people like about this one so

much? I personally think it's because it's full of positive

vibes and a beautiful, poetic writing that describes how

God is with us. In the majority of his Psalms where he

talks about God protecting people, he does so in a

depressing-ass tone. He starts off by talking about how

down-in-the-dumps he is and how everybody is crushing

him and out to rip his heart out..." But even though I'm

close to breathing my last breath and dying at the hands

of evil and wicked people, I know you will save me." With

this Psalm, he focuses on God from start to finish. He

paints a picture of how a walk with God is like a beautiful

day at the beach. A day that will never end, even if

people try and rain on your parade.

12. **Psalm 42:** If I had to pick a Psalm where he completely opens up but is completely depressing as fuck it would have to be this one. The first line sounds good where he says he thirsts for God like he thirsts or desires for anything else in the entire world. After Line 1, the rest is all downhill. He now focuses on how God has left him, God can't be found, God is gone, why has God forsaken me and why has God watched him cry so hard, that his body is dehydrated. It was weird to hear him go so hard about God supposedly leaving him; *especially* after every Psalm I've read prior to this where he may have been in a dark place, but he still took time to dedicate at least the last section to praising God for being faithful. This time, he never says that *he* will continue to trust in God; instead, he tells *us* to keep *our* hope in God. His last line is simply, "God is my God."

13. **Psalm 91:** This is my favorite Psalm and is so powerful, I am going to take the time to write the entire Psalm out

for you…edited for the sake of time and space of course. Here it is:

- **"If you trust in God, He will be more than just your shelter, He will be your fortress!"** When you talk about shelter, that's like a house, condo or apartment. "Home Sweet Home" is a safe place for anybody BUT David said if you trust completely in God, you will sleep super-safe and at peace and that it will be like sleeping in a fortress. A fortress isn't like a house. A fortress has thick-ass walls, guards circling it 24/7/365, 6-inch-thick steel doors and bullet-proof windows! THAT'S the difference between trusting in anything or anyone else versus trusting in God.

- **If you get caught in a snare…God will get you out of it!"** It doesn't matter what kind of shit you get into…God will get you out of it!

- **"No kind of sickness or disease will affect you!"**

- **"Nothing that scares people at night will scare you".** Anybody that hides in the dark to rob people or take advantage of people at nighttime will not be able to sneak up on you or hurt you.

- **"If 1,000 people fall to your left and right because of disease or anything else, you will still be standing."** No matter how many people are dying around you from disease or as a result of being punished by God or because of ANYTHING...your ass will be unaffected and still standing.

- **"NO harm will overtake you!"**

- **"NO disaster will come near your tent!"** Any type of criminal activity like break-ins or some shit like that will pass right by you in your fortress.

- **"For He will command His angels concerning you..."** All of that protection will be the result of

God keeping an eye on you as well as Guardian angels who will watch every step you take. Angels are *extremely* powerful beings, capable of destroying entire cities by hand in one day. I saw a video where the world's richest people felt safe because they have a couple of bodyguards. Floyd "Money" Mayweather says all his bodyguards have to be at least 275 pounds and over 6 feet tall. Really? David says God will protect us with angels! There is no bodyguard on Earth that can stand against an angel!

- **"You will kill lions and serpents!"** The lion is a symbol of raw, wild strength and the serpent is the image of being slick. David is letting us know that no matter how strong or slick somebody is, if they are trying to fuck with you...it won't go down like they think it will!

- **"He says because God loves you He will protect you, always answer you, be with you during hard times and will let you live a long, satisfying life."**

This the last Psalm I will talk about for two reasons. The 1st reason is because 99% of his Psalms are similar in nature. This does not mean they aren't significant, different and beautiful in their own way, it's just that they share the same basic template.

They all show how David loved God so much, that he came to God for everything whether he was in a good or bad mood. He wasn't afraid to tell God when he felt like God didn't care about him. The amazing part is he felt equally as comfortable giving God credit for protecting him and staying with him through thick and thin.

The 2nd reason is because I want to end the chapter about Psalm with the powerful words of reassurance and confidence that, in my view, portray God's protective power and David's absolute confidence in that power. These words are brought to life a lot more when you look at all of the extreme situations David credits God with pulling him through.

David has first-hand experience on being delivered, rescued, supported, loved, disciplined and provided for by God. So, when someone like *that* is describing to us how God will act in our lives if we trust Him, his words hold weight like a mutha fucka!

The next chapter is by David's son King Solomon. It is primarily wise sayings, no songs. He doesn't have the ups and downs from a life of combat his dad had, but he speaks from his personal experiences with having a dad who slept with a married woman and killed her husband, how to build wealth and keep it and how to use the power of Wisdom to your full advantage like he did. Check it out…

<u>CHAPTER TWO</u>

Proverbs

The book of Proverbs is written by King Solomon, son of

King David. Before we go over his wise writings from Proverbs, I

want to introduce you to his first request from God as well as the

first case, involving two prostitutes and a dead baby, that he had

to pass judgement on as acting King.

When he was about to take the throne, God asked

Solomon if he could have one thing from Him, whatever he

wanted, what would it be? At this point in time, he is in his early

teens. Without hesitation he asks for wisdom.

God said, "Excellent choice! Most people in your position

would have asked for some sexxxy girls or a ton of money. Since

you only asked for wisdom, as long as you have the throne, you will be the richest king on the planet *and* I will give you all the girls and wealth you can handle. I will also give you great honor."

The next day his wisdom is tested. Two prostitutes and a young baby are brought before him. The first prostitute states her case.

She says, "King Solomon, me and my roommate, I mean my *ex*-roommate, lived alone in a house. I had a baby and 3 days later she had a baby. *Her* baby died in the middle of the night. While I was sleeping, she did the old switch-a-roo and put her dead baby in my bed!

I know this because when I woke up in the morning to nurse my baby, I was sad that my baby died until...until I looked at the baby in the light. Once I looked at the baby up close and saw it wasn't mine, I was like, 'I know this bitch didn't switch our babies?!' Sorry about cussing your honor..."

The second woman can't take it anymore and just interrupts the first lady. "You're just mad because your baby died. How dare you lie on me in front of this entire court! I may be a prostitute but one thing I ain't is a liar!" King Solomon is watching them and lets them go back and forth a little bit before rendering his verdict.

"Does anybody have a sword? Okay, good. You, guard with the sword, grab the baby and cut it in half. You know, like right down the middle from head to toe. Since they can't decide, they can each have half a baby."

The first mother breaks down and cries, "Please don't kill it! Give it to her so it will stay alive…"

The ex-roommate is a little more heartless about the situation and tells the King, "Yeah, that's fair. If I can't have the baby, nobody will!"

Solomon orders the baby to be given to the first woman. It became crystal clear to him that it was her baby because her protective mother instincts and love for her child were so strong, she would rather see the baby in the arms of another woman than having it die.

And that is the young man who wrote 99.99% of some of the wisest and simplest sayings in the book of Proverbs. If I had to summarize them, I would say he focused the need to have wisdom in these categories: females, partying, building wealth and...probably females again. He is a good one to take advice from in all these categories. As King, he had like 800 wives and was the richest King alive.

There is another very interesting point I would like to make about his sayings. A lot of them are warnings for the men about women. Not just any women. He was specifically telling men to watch out for cheating wives.

If you remember, his dad, King David, had looked at a married woman, knew she was married and still had sex with her, got her pregnant, had her husband killed and then married her; only to have the baby get sick and die. That lady was Solomon's mother and the baby that died was his big brother.

That's another powerful thing about the Bible. We are able to see intimate details of people's lives that we can learn from and possibly relate to on a high level. There are many people in the world with mommy and/or daddy issues. I believe Solomon, one of the wisest and wealthiest Kings to walk the Earth, was still human and experienced a lot of the everyday things we experience.

He used his personal experiences and incredible gift from God of wisdom to share warnings and lessons with us that were written thousands of years ago that are still very relevant. Here are a select handful of his proverbs in *his* words with my extra commentaries in *my* words:

1. **Proverbs 1:** The first Proverb is a fitting one because it starts off with a father's advice to his son. The main points are that you shouldn't hang out with people who like to rob, steal and get scam people. If somebody approaches you with a way to get money in a scandalous way, tell him no, no matter how good it sounds. He said people who like to just sit around and figure out ways to get money and wealth by any means necessary are idiots...so dumb that they don't even recognize their scams are obvious as shit. I have to tell you something on a personal note here. I have a function on my cellie that screens callers. If the phone number is strange in any kind of way, the screen will say, "Scam Likely" as the caller's i.d. Every once in a while, my curiosity gets the best of me and I answer. "Yo, this better be good," I answer. "Yes, my name is Shirley. Is this Hector?" Sometimes I'm rude and will say, "Do I sound like my mutha fuckin' name is Hector?! Leave me the fuck alone and stop scamming, bitch!!" and then I hang up, if she hasn't hung up already. Other times I am more polite and will

say, "Yo, this better be good" and the person on the other end of the line will say, "Hello, my name is Richard and I'm looking for Jason." I respond politely with, "No. You have the wrong number, sir" and that's where the slick shit kicks in. "Oh, well that's actually okay if you're not Jason because I have an offer that you can take advantage of..." I cut him off with, "I just said I wasn't Jason! Leave me the fuck alone and lose this number, bitch!" There's something about people who make random phone calls or send emails that ask for help or that try and look official so you will respond to a scam. I email them back and say, "Dear scammer. I am down with Jesus and I have important shit to do and you are bothering both His time and mine. Because you are a piece of shit and have nothing better to do than this dumb ass scam, I'm going to do something special for you. I'm going to personally ask Jesus if He can destroy all your finances and any scam you are involved with and even your health until you get on your knees and apologize to God. And my name is Larry Yff. I want you to know exactly who did this to you. Enjoy your day."

Now I know I got off track by a page or two, but I like to make some of this old shit Solomon talked about relevant. The actual proverb starts off with, "My son, if sinful men entice you, do not give in to them." If I told my sons or any young buck I was mentoring to, "avoid sinful men that may entice thee…" I would get absolutely nowhere. First off, they would be asking me "what the fuck does entice mean" and secondly, that shit sounds old and retarded, like a lot of Bible scriptures. I don't know if people really talked like that back then or if Bible publishers just want to make it sound super-holy. Whatever the reason, please stop. Okay, that's enough of me rambling…let's get to the next Proverb…oh, wait. The end of this proverb is good because it tells us if we don't pay attention and learn as soon as possible, Wisdom will leave us and laugh at us. Solomon often personified Wisdom as though it were a wise person. It's a cool thing he does and it helped me view wisdom as someone who can give me advice;

instead of just being a thing, a saying. That may work for you and it may not. I'm just putting this shit out here for you to digest however you want…

2. Proverbs 3: I LOVE how he describes Wisdom here! It is artistic, beautiful, true, poetic and the shit makes perfect sense. Check it out*…"Blessed are those who find wisdom and gain understanding. She is more profitable than silver and yields better returns than gold. She is more precious than rubies; nothing you desire can compare to her. Long life is in her right hand; in her left hand are riches and honor. Her ways are pleasant and all her paths are peace. She is a tree of life to those who keep her close. It was with wisdom that God laid the Earth's foundation and set the heavens in place. God used wisdom to divide the bodies of water into lakes and rivers and made the clouds drop rain water from the sky."* Beautiful…

3. Proverbs 5: This is the first of many proverbs that warns the fella's to keep an eye out for certain kinds of women. I'll give you his words first, and then I'll give it to you how regular people talk. His words: *"For the lips of the adulterous woman drip honey and her speech is smoother than oil; but in the end her words taste bitter and are sharp as a double-edged sword. Her feet go down to death. Her steps lead straight to the grave. She gives no thought to the way of life; her path wanders aimlessly, but she does not know it. My sons, listen to me and don't turn away from what I say. Keep to a path far from her, do not go near the door of her house or you will lose your honor to others and your dignity to one who is cruel, lest strangers feast on your wealth and enrich the house of another. At the end of your life, you will groan when your flesh and body are spent. You will say, 'How I hated discipline! How my heart spurned correction! I would not obey my teachers.' Drink water* *from your own well. Let them be yours alone, never to be shared with strangers. May your fountain be blessed and may you enjoy the wife of your youth, who is loving and graceful like a deer. May her breasts satisfy you always, may you ever be intoxicated with her love. Why, my son, be intoxicated with another man's wife? Why embrace the bosom of a wayward woman?"* That was pretty deep and beautiful, huh? Listen, I am not saying I don't like the way some of this shit is written. But I *am* saying it makes it difficult for me to follow sometimes. I get the message and trust me, all of his warnings about certain ways of females are extremely accurate. It's just when it has all the, "thy ways dost leadeth to" and "why shalt thine eyes fail thee" that I get like, "fuck it." Anyways, he was talking about females who are married and cheat on their husbands. He says the way they talk to you is very smooth and enticing and with just her words she can draw you in. in the end, he is correct when he relates your best outcome from sleeping with a married to death. There is absolutely nothing good that can come from it. Her husband could find out and try to kill you or you can get somebody's wife pregnant and now you have to come out your pocket with abortion money, she has to try and say the baby is her husband's or now you have to try and get along her husband and you *know* that nigga hates you and wants you dead. Visitation days and holidays are gonna be stressful than a mutha fucka if you keep that baby. I love how he ends the proverb by telling you what you should be doing instead of being laid up with some other dude's wife. He says you should be finding some young lady you meet while you're young and marry her. He says you two should have fun sex and be so in love that both of you walk around glowing! He then ends it with, "...she should be yours alone..." It's as if to say, if you had a wife, would you want to share her with anybody? Before we go to the next chapter, once again, I want to add something personal. For me, this gives you a chance to see these old-ass, wise-ass sayings being applied to our times. This proverb actually was one of the major parts of the Bible that helped me get focused and out of my cocaine and porn addictions. When I would spend an entire paycheck smoking crack, or sniffing coke and watching porn or feeling up some random stripper or her feeling me up, I wouldn't feel anything real in the moment until *after* the moment. It was exactly like Solomon described it when he talked about "losing your honor to others and your dignity to those who are cruel." I wasn't fucking around with married women, but the fantasy mix of cocaine and strippers or porno made me lose my honor and dignity. I lost my honor because nobody respected me. Hell, I didn't totally respect me. I couldn't keep my word and I was just a crack-head, loser who only cared about getting high and having fantasy sex. I definitely "lost my dignity to those who are cruel." I can't call them cruel because they were just doing what they chose to do to make money, but the guys I would get my drugs from would offer me work that was in my area of expertise at extremely cheap prices or for drugs. They didn't care about my addiction or why I started getting high in the first place. And in their defense, that really isn't something that should concern them. All they were concerned with was getting cheap labor or keeping me close so I could spend all my money with them. Sometimes, the jobs were degrading, but I needed to keep cool with them to keep the drugs coming…so I would do the work they requested at the price they set. It made me feel low as fuck. Sub-human. No dignity. Doing work for someone you buy drugs from, or having a job and spending your checks on drugs is humiliating. Solomon posed the question, "Why should someone else feast on your wealth and make *his* life better off your lustful ways that you can't control?" When I got high, I instantly had to have porn videos playing on my phone or some female stripping for me or anything fantasy-sex related. Reading what Solomon said struck home with me because in my lustful pursuit to "enjoy" fantasy sex for a couple hours or days was making my dope dealers rich. They were driving around in new cars and clothes from the profits made off my dumb ass. I've had many "episodes" that were big enough to pay one of their house and car notes. In fact, one of the guys I was buying from pulled up to meet me and bring me my drugs and I didn't recognize him at first…he was in a new F-150 pickup. These words from Solomon were a wake-up call for me to start getting my lustful ways in order so I could start respecting myself, regaining my dignity and keeping money in my pocket. I listened to him because I read his life and how he dealt with females who lead him off track. Towards the end of his life, he got so off track because of females that, even though he built God a huge, gold-covered temple, he began to let these foreign women he was having sex with, convince him to use his great wealth to build elaborate temples to the idols and gods they were worshipping. If you just skim through his proverbs, I'll bet there will be something that rings true. It may not be the exact situation he describes, but the end lesson may be useful for you. I wasn't sexxxxing married females, but the main chaos of what he talked about regarding uncontrolled lust for woman was being played out in my life in a devastating way and his warnings were still good advice for me. Moving on...

4. Proverbs 7: He follows Proverbs 5 up with another wise lesson about sleeping with a married woman. I just wanted to show you, in his words, how he describes a young man he was watching who was out and about when a cheating wife approached him and got him to come home with her. He describes the scene as, **"...a cow going to the slaughter, a deer stuck in a trap until the hunter check's his trap and puts an arrow through its' heart and like a bird who is flying around freely and unaware it is about to fly straight into a trap and die."**

5. Proverbs 20: This proverb is a typical one that hits on multiple subjects. This one talks about beer, being lazy, love and receiving inheritance money.

- **"Drinking beer makes you want to fight and act stupid and if you let beer control you, you're a fool."** If you've ever been to a bar or a college party, you had to have seen a drunken bar scene that included two drunk people arguing over something stupid and either fighting or thinking they were fighting. A lot of times they are just swinging and missing and looking stupid and drunk.

- **"A King's anger is as terrifying as a lion's roar. If the roar is directed at you, you could lose your life."** You don't want to get on the bad side of your superior like a supervisor or boss.

- **"Smart people avoid strife, but fools love it."** It's smart to stay out of certain fights and arguments.

Foolish people don't know the difference and always end up in the middle of bullshit.

- **"The sluggard doesn't plow his field; but looks for gain in the time of harvest."** People who are lazy have all kinds of excuses for why they can't work, but they still expect everything to be taken care of for them.

- **"Love not sleep, lest thou come to poverty."** People who like to sleep a lot and sleep in tend to be poor. He warns against just lying around all day sleeping, playing video games or channel surfing for hours.

- **"An inheritance may be gotten hastily at the beginning, but it will not be blessed at the end."** He's telling us that people love to receive money from an inheritance but if they aren't used to having money or have always had it given to them, in the end it could be a disaster. On a

personal note, I know of several people who have

received money from an inheritance and it was

gone within two years. Oh, I recently watched a

documentary by some rich kid who was rich

because his great, great grandpa was rich as fuck.

I'm thinking his great, great grandpa started

Johnson & Johnson medical company. He decided

to do a tell-all video about the affects of growing

up with a financial value of millions of dollars and

not appreciating the value of money and wealth.

He interviewed a bunch of super-rich friends he

grew up with to get their view on this. It was

crazy! Kid #1 said his family was worth billions but

he was told from the start, if he didn't work for

the family company, he wouldn't be getting shit!

Kid #2 had a dad who owned casinos. He was a

cocky, unattractive kid who liked to brag about his

family's wealth. He said, "Yeah, you know like, when some average-ass kid tries and talks shit to me, it's like I wanna just say, 'Dude. Shut the fuck up! I have enough family to buy your entire family.'" This Kid did drugs and got drunk his entire college "career". He admitted he literally attended class about 6 times during the year. His dad knew the President of the school so he just passed him to stay on the dad's good side. He was a complete prick. You could see it in the way he talked and walked. Kid #3 asked his dad why he didn't like to talk about money and his dad said it's just not polite and should be avoided at all costs. This advice was coming from a man who literally never leaves the family mansion, has never worked a day in his life because he's been living off of his inheritance, is scared to be around people and just sits in the house all day reading newspapers and painting pretty pictures. When this kid asked his dad what he should do in the future to find his purpose, the dad said, "Well, you will never be broke, so why don't you just travel and study things like birds or maps of major cities?" What the fuck?? Kid #4 was taught to sign a prenuptial agreement at a young age to make sure no female could take his money. When he turned 18, he received, as he put it, "an annual income in the high six-figures" that he's supposed to continue to receive for life. He did every drug on the planet and dropped out of college to work in Mexico on a farm or some shit. He had no idea what to do with his life and that was a very common theme. Kid #5, when asked what she wanted to do in life, said, "I really don't know. Maybe I'll ride horses or become a lawyer..." Her answer was cut short because she was being interviewed while she was walking through some high-priced store and she started talking about all the purses she had. "I don't look at the price. It's scary. I do know they each cost several thousands of dollars. Isn't this one cute? I'll buy it! I mean, my mom is going to totally flip-out when she gets my credit card bill! She'll pay it and then get over it..." Her interview ended with us not knowing what the fuck she wanted to do in life other than add to her already extensive purse collection.

6. **Proverbs 31:** This is the last proverb we will look at. I like, as usual, all the different topics it covers. I also like how the lessons and words of wisdom about drinking and women come from a co-author who is a female.

- She warns the men to not be foolish and give their strength to women.

- She says Kings and Rulers don't drink. She said save that type of shit for people who want to be depressed in life, drink their problems away or who want to die an early death.

- She says the men should make sure they find a good wife and not settle for just any old female. A good wife is worth more than any jewels. She will have the ability to help run the family businesses outside of the house as well as make sure the house is a home. She will take care of the children, the family and her husband faithfully. She will stay up late if she has to, in order to make sure her family has what it needs. Looks and her standing in society aren't important things to consider when looking for a wife. The right woman will be beautiful in her own way and will create her own position in life.

If she has any type of income, put some of it into the family bank and make sure she gets to take some of the money she made with her own hands and do her thing with it. It will bring more wealth to the family.

With all the hype by the media trying to paint a picture of the family structure differently than the way God designed it, I thought it was fitting to make this the last proverb I cover. It allowed me to end this chapter on a positive note about what a family structure should look like and how it should operate.

In the end, King Solomon did what he saw his dad do: write down and share what God has done in his life for the world to see. His emphasis was based on cheating wives, wealth and power because that's what he knew and was familiar with.

The next chapter covers the next book he is credited with writing. If you like money, want money, need money, have wealth, want more wealth or any combination of those, pay close

attention to this next book.

CHAPTER THREE

Ecclesiastes

This book is a weird one. It only has 12 chapters. That's not what makes it weird. What makes it weird is that it's a book written by the wealthiest King of his day who has everything he wants; yet he talks about how life has no meaning. He has the most artistic and beautiful way of saying, "Life is shit. We're all fucked. We're all gonna die." How does that happen?

On one hand, he can have any and everything power and money can give; while on the other hand, all that material shit can't stop him from dying. There is a gloomy, depressing feel to this book, with the creative wording and style being the only thing giving it life.

He provides advice about wealth and money management that all the top money managers, financial institutions and financial advisors follow even though it was written thousands of years ago.

Check out the clips from this book on the meaning and purpose of wealth and life from his view...

1. **Ecclesiastes 1:** This chapter starts off with a couple of questions on life that have the wise King under the belief that it doesn't matter what you do because nothing really changes or matters. Here they are for you to think about:

   - When one generation ends, the next one starts; when that one ends, the next one starts...

   - The sun rises and sets, the next day it does the exact same thing and the next day and the next...

   - The water from the rivers flows into the lakes, but the lakes never fill up. Water from the lake's surface goes up into the clouds, only to be returned to Earth in the form of rain, back into the rivers…

- Whatever happens in the present becomes the past and is soon forgotten. Whatever will happen in the future will become the present, then the past and it will also be forgotten soon.

- He ends this chapter with the question: Is there really anything new that happens on the Earth? When I stopped and answered this question for myself, I was like, "Shit. What he's saying is about right." It didn't depress me or no shit like that, but it did make me wonder what it was about my life, right here today in the present, that I could do to make a difference? I had a couple of people I knew that got shot and killed. I look back and remember everybody being shook up and talking about how their memory will live on forever. I remember all the anger, emotion and tears.

Within 3 months, conversations about all the victims were almost non-existent, with their memories being limited to t-shirts or in the hearts of their immediate family members. Anyone outside of that circle seemed to forget about the incidents over time. I was 15 years old when Tupac got killed. He's the most famous musical artist on the planet and every show, every commercial, every talk-show around the world was talking about it. Once again, within about 3 months, the conversation shifted from Tupac's death to some other new artist on the rise or some political hot-button issue of the day. My point is, yes, people and things come and go and I see how Solomon could feel that way; but when people like him and his dad, King David, and even people like me and you really follow God's laws, history is made in such a way that the world can never be the same. That's my personal goal.

2. **Ecclesiastes 2:** In his search for purpose and understanding in life, King Solomon decides to go out and do whatever the fuck his wealth and power allow him to do. He does whatever his heart desires and takes whatever he lays his eyes on. He then gives us a list of all the shit he did and concludes it with, "I did all this shit and got all this stuff, for what? When I die, it will be left for somebody else to enjoy or tear-down." He was even kind of depressed about all the wisdom he had gained over the years because, in his eyes all that didn't matter either because he was going to die, just like any fool on the street. What follows is his impressive list to find the meaning of life in things:

- He built great "works", whatever the fuck that means

- He built huge vineyards

- He built huge houses

- He planted gardens and orchards that had every tree and plant in them known to mankind

- He gathered tons of silver, gold and the most priceless and expensive treasures from around the world

- He ended this proverb on a surprisingly cheerful note and said, "In the end, I have discovered that the most joy I've found in life was when I was able to simply have a nice meal and be able to do whatever work it is that makes my soul happy." Now *that's* an amazing conclusion! He went around and had famous singers sing for him, he built all the lavish shit and bought shit and built shit and all that shit didn't mean as much as a nice, home-cooked meal in the comfort of good old, Home Sweet Home...

3. **Ecclesiastes 3:** Some of the most famous quotes about the proper use of time come from this proverb. Time is something we all have an equal amount of. How we use it is what makes the difference. If I was to sum it all up for you, I would say,

"There is a time, place and purpose for everything." That doesn't do this proverb justice so I will lay it out for you:

- A time to die and a time to be born. Death is an essential part of life. If nobody died, the Earth would be overcrowded and the resources would run out from human and animal consumption. Face death as an oddly beautiful part of your life, because it will happen to everyone.

- A time to plant and a time to harvest your crop. Life has seasons like farming. First you have to do the work of planting your seeds. Then you have to water and fertilize the growing crop until the season to harvest it comes. This process involves patience because you can't rush the growth of any crop.

- A time to get and a time to lose. You aren't going to win every time at everything in life. Be prepared to win some and lose some.

- A time to love and a time to hate. There will eventually be some things in life you don't like. Nobody ever has or ever will just be in love with everything.

- A time for peace and a time for war. God is a God of war and His advice on war was, "Try to negotiate peace, but if you can't agree on peace, then it's time to go to war."

- A time to keep shit and a time to get rid of shit. Some people like to hoard things from friends to shoes. At some point you will run out of physical space or emotional space. At that point, you will have to start getting rid of some shit. Some friends may not be meant to go into your next chapter in life, for example.

- A time to talk and a time to shut the fuck up. People who talk a lot don't learn because they haven't taken the time to listen. Once you have listened and learned is when you become qualified to start talking and

teaching. Until then, shut the fuck up.

- The last thing there is time for is to, once again, 1)

  enjoy some good food in a safe environment and 2) be

  able to enjoy the work you have done and are doing in

  life.

4. **Ecclesiastes 11:** This financial lesson has the keys for financial

wealth and money management that all the pros on Wall

Street and the other financial centers of the universe swear

by. Many investors try and take credit for the lessons you are

about to see in this writing from King Solomon. He said this

shit thousands of years ago and they were recorded, saved

and put into the Bible for safe-keeping. I took the opportunity

to list and summarize for them for you:

- **"Cast thy bread upon the waters, for thou shalt find it

  after many days."** I didn't know they called money

  "bread" back in Solomon's day? Interesting. Just

kidding. I think he used the water metaphor because

when you put something on top of the water, the

waves take it wherever the fuck they want to.

Whatever you set on the water gets scattered

everywhere. If you take this and relate it to investing,

it means you should take your money and invest it in

many different things. He says you might think it's

scattered and lost but it's not. It appears that way, but

in reality, when your investment period is over, you

will get it back with interest.

- **"Give a portion to 7 or 8 different things because you don't know what evil is on the Earth."** He says the same thing as he did in the first verse, except he gives us the reason why it's important to diversify your investment portfolio: you don't know what the fuck is going to happen tomorrow. If you invest all your money in oil and the oil market plummets, you will lose all of your investment money. If you invest all your

money in technology stocks and they start to lose

value, once again, you will lose all your money. Based

on this very important investment principle, financial

advisors love to advertise how they are experts at

diversifying investments. They know that is the only

known strategy to guarantee the investor will not lose

everything...unless every, single stock market on the

planet collapses at once. Solomon likes to make

references to nature. When he made the statement,

"...you don't know what evil is on the Earth..." as a

reason to diversify your investment portfolio. To

explain that in more detail he adds a couple of

metaphors. He says, "You don't know when it's going

to rain" to let you know you have no control over the

weather. Let's say you are investing in crops. You

need to diversify your money because there may be a

drought, flooding or the proper amount of rain. If it

floods or there is a drought, your entire investment money will be lost. He also mentions how a tree falls, saying, "You can't predict which way a tree will fall or when it will fall" as if to say there are things out there that you cannot predict or control.

- **"He that observeth the wind shall not sow and he that regardeth the clouds shall not reap."** Excellent investment points. Sowing is a process of planting something, just like investing is the process of "planting" your money somewhere. If a farmer doesn't plant his seeds because he is busy worrying about whether or not the wind will blow his seeds away or whether there might not be enough rain to water them and make the seeds grow will wind up not investing in anything. His investment tip is: Don't try and wait for the right time and don't try and predict whether or not your investment will grow because there will never be a perfect time to invest and you can't predict the growth of any investment. Just invest and invest in as many different areas you can.

- **"In the morning sow your seed and at nighttime don't withhold your hand."** Here he is telling you to go ahead and invest. You can't predict anything about investing. And once you do invest, don't be scared to check on them at the end of the day. Some may have risen and some may have fallen or maybe they all have risen in value.

The book of Ecclesiastes seems to me to be a book on him reflecting about life. This is a powerful and wealthy king who was given the throne. He did nothing to earn it. He didn't wage war or cause an uprising and kill the ruling King. He was simply born and inherited it when his dad died.

When I referenced the documentary about the rich kids, there were lots of similarities to King Solomon's life. He inherited his position and wealth, similar to the rich kids. Some of them were so confused as to the responsibility of such a large inheritance, they felt guilty and wanted to escape from it somehow.

In his writing, he says, "If you're not careful with an inheritance, you can fuck it up and be in worse shape than you were before your received it." A lot of his ecclesiastical writings reflect the depression and reflection that comes with receiving something for nothing.

This book shows his deepest thoughts and emotions. I suppose at some point when you can have whatever you want and everything is given to you, you probably do begin to wonder about what else is out there. You have wealth without working for it. People envy you but have no idea what all the pressures are that come with wealth. Like Big Poppa said, "Mo' money, mo' problems."

It was cool to see him put it all on the line for the world to read. I could see his depression, anxiety and his joy. It was as though he took a page out of his dad's book of Psalm, saw the effect it had, and gave it a shot.

Regarding wealth, if an insanely wealthy king is telling you how to invest and other investment tips...follow them to the letter.

<u>SUMMARY</u>

Summarizing this book takes me on an emotional rollercoaster. King David was constantly going from praising God to borderline cursing Him. There were some of his writings that eloquently and picturesquely described both the love he had for God as well as the love God has for him. In his next breath, he is asking God why He has left him. He's depressed because everybody is trying to kill and attack him and the next line, he talks about how he's not worried about shit because God has his back.

Then there's Solomon. His writing style is similar to his dad's. He isn't afraid to open up and share anything emotional that is going on in his life. His book of Proverb is full of warnings and advice that, even though the topic may be considered dark, have a light tone to them.

Not Ecclesiastes. That book starts off dark and stayed dark. One of the darkest, but most reflective books I've ever read. Even though the entire book was reflecting on how there is nothing to really live for in life and that life kind of actually sucks, in his eyes. The only positive moments were when he talked about the promise of a return on investments and enjoying a nice meal in the comfort of your own space.

The whole ride for me of these two kings was informative and heartbreaking. It was heartbreaking to feel the despair in their writings. As a person who used to have a couple of addictions, I can relate.

On the flipside, there were enough bright moments that were based on God's love to balance any and all of the depressed and lonely moments the father and son authors faced.

I try and open up, and show others how to open up, about emotional places we go to or questions we deal with in private. The next section Private Matters is my way of putting it all out there for the world to read and possibly relate and learn from.

PRIVATE MATTERS

This section is in the back of every book in the series. It is a mixed bunch of "essays" that show different views on issues that people only talk about in private, kind of like the topic of this book, making them Private Matters topics. Take a look:

LOVE LANGUAGE OF CHRISTIANS

I am married and me and my wife love God and we love sex. We like to fuck or make love. We don't like to have sexual intercourse. Does that mean we don't love God? Since we made sure we legalized our marriage in a church before God, does using the word "fuck" mean we have disrespected our sexual marriage vows to God? If we love God, does that mean we are supposed to use King James talk when it comes to bedroom talk? I don't believe so.

How are Christians supposed to talk when it comes to sex and love? That is a question that should be debated and discussed in the church. But the church doesn't know how to talk about it...so I will.

Before I was married, I used to tell females, "Yes, I want you to suck my dick." I NEVER said, "yes, I would like it if you put my penis in your mouth and receive oral sex from you." I NEVER just pulled my dick out and kind of smiled at her and looked from her mouth to my dick and back to her mouth hoping she would get the idea that I want my dick sucked. I openly said it then and now that I am married, I have to be just as open with her and vice versa.

If my wife just sat there with her legs open waiting for me to suck on her clit without a formal invitation…that shit ain't happenin'. She needs to feel free to express what she wants. I take that back. Actually, when you're married, there is a beautiful code you establish and nothing needs to be said. When I pull my dick out and lay back and smile at her, she knows what to do. When she lays with her legs open and raises her right eyebrow, I know what to do.

Now that I'm married, does that mean I can never say to my wife, "The kids are gone for the night, so you know we 'bout to get our fuck on all over the house. I want you to walk around naked so I can look at your sexxxy ass all day and when I can't take it anymore, I'm gonna grab you, turn you around, bend you over and fuck the shit out of you." Is that how married Christians are supposed to talk? Is that permissible

Christian language?

Some of you may think I'm disgusting and that I am not a

good Christian because I want to fuck my sexxxxy wife instead

of wanting to "have sexual intercourse with my wife."

Some of you may think I'm disgusting and that I am not a

good Christian because I want to lick my wife's pussy until she

cums instead of wanting to "lick her in her clitoral/vaginal

region until she reaches a climax."

Some of you may think I'm disgusting and that I am not a

good Christian because I openly tell my wife to "turn around

and put your ass in my face so I can kiss it. I think you have a

sexxxy ass and I can't keep my mutha fuckin' lips and tongue

off of that sexxxy thang" instead of openly telling my wife

"Can you please turn around? I really like your buttocks and I

would like it if you would bend over in front of me so I can kiss it. I just love the sight and feel of your rear end so much that I can't stop kissing all over it."

The point I am trying to make is that I don't believe you have to go all King James in the bedroom when you have sex as a Christian, married couple. God made sex to be enjoyable. One of the authors in the Bible said to the men, "get married to the woman you fall in love with as a youth and enjoy her breasts…" Another author in the Bible said, "the marriage bed is sacred and something for a husband and wife to enjoy however they see fit."

If that's really true, if my wife and I are used to talking a certain love language before we were married, we should feel free to talk in that same language as a married couple if that is the language that makes us comfortable, keeps our sex life strong and keeps us faithful to each other.

If I'm married and have sexual desires that I can't express to my wife, I am going to be inclined to hit the strip clubs and bars more frequently so I can come across a female who "understands" me and who I can enjoy having sex with. Since marriage is a thing that God supports and created as the power-base of society, we need to be talking about these things BEFORE marriage.

At the same time, there has to be boundaries and limits. Just because I may want to have anal sex with my wife does not mean she has to comply and take it every week in her ass. We still have to compromise. Maybe she takes it like that on Valentine's Day, President's Day and our anniversary or something. That's for you two to decide.

My point is that it's your marriage and your sex life. The point is, you two need to talk about sex or your marriage will fall the fuck apart. If you're a guy and secretly want to have sex with other guys, that's some shit your wife needs to know

BEFORE you get married. We should all be at the point where we can share our views on sex and decide whether or not to move on together or get off the train.

Sex is an important element of marriage that needs to be talked about. When I look back at the people in my church when I was growing up, I can tell you that there was only one couple, and I won't say who it is, that looked like they were having sex. All the rest of the married couples looked like zombies. I never saw anybody sneak and hold hands or saw a couple share a laugh with another couple and the wife blush and kiss her husband on the cheek.

I went to an all-white church and that's what I saw. Anytime I went to white churches, that is the vibe I got. I have to go a step further and say I got the same vibe from all-black churches as well.

My experience with church and sex was that it never happened until...until somebody got a divorce because the wife was cheating or the husband had a full-blown porn addiction that was out of control. There was a pastor who committed suicide because he was hooked on phone sex and spending hundreds of dollars a month. He felt guilty and felt like he couldn't share that with anybody. Kirk Franklin, a famous gospel singer, came out and said he had a major porn addiction. He had porn videos stashed all around the house behind every television or something crazy like that. It happens. It happens to anybody and it needs to be talked about. It's major incidents like that when you realized people in the church had sex problems or were actually having sex.

I have to add this to be fair, Joel Osteen has a wife who looks like she wants to have fun sexually, she's attractive and dresses in a modern, conservative-yet-sexxxy style. That's refreshing to see. Her husband Joel on the other hand, with his perfectly set and sprayed hair style, bleached white teeth

with that permanent smile on his face and that joyful message

he delivers every Sunday, looks like he could care less whether

they had sex or not. I mean, they do have a couple of kids as

proof, but other than that...you can tell Joe ain't really hittin'

that like he's supposed to.

There is a twist to all of this. When I was in church, it was

also the place where I saw plenty of sexxxxy females. An older

friend of mine used to tell me that church was the best place

to find a nice female. I think he must have been talking to a

lot of church-going females as well because the single ladies in

church had a tendency to dress sexxxy; unlike the married

females who tended to want to leave the impression that they

were sanctified, highly favored, blessed and content to be

married.

It's unreal for us to think a pastor doesn't get turned on by

females outside of his wife. If he didn't, that means he is either into homosexual activity (and should not be in the pulpit) or he is in complete denial of his maleness.

I've asked a couple preachers about this and even though they were married, they still say they see women as being attractive and even sexxxy. They even admitted to me that they still look at a sexxxy female walking by sometimes. For them though, they say the difference is their thought process: just because they are married doesn't mean they don't see or recognize female beauty...it just means they understand how serious marriage is and straying from his wife for some sex is not worth falling out of favor with God, destroying a marriage, destroying the power-base of the family structure, causing emotional harm to the kids and a bunch of other chaos that results from lacking sexual discipline.

If you think I'm being unrealistic, feel free to look around your church and see how many couples look like they are having fun sexually. Look at your pastor and his wife and see if you think he is hittin' it from the back and they are enjoying doing the reverse-cowgirl position or doing 69's.

When I look around congregations, I see plenty of sexxxy women I would like to have sex with (this of course is before I was married). What I don't see is married couples looking sexually satisfied; especially the pastor. Nine out of ten times the pastor's wife has a dress that drags down to her ankles and a shirt that's long-sleeved and buttoned all the way to the top button…looking like she walked straight off the television show Bonanza, Little House on the Prairie or some other old-school show.

Do I want my pastor's wife wearing short, sexxxy skirts with high heels and a short top so her ass shows? No. I'm not saying that. What I am saying is that when a person is having fun sexually, it shows in the way they walk, talk and dress and it would be nice to see a pastor-wife team looking like they are human and like they like sex.

In the end, I think, as one who was sexually irresponsible and a Christian for many years, that it's important that the church grow some balls and takes a stand on sexuality. Everybody else openly pushes their thoughts and agenda for sex.

People involved with homosexual activity have openly let it be known that they want to teach public school kids at early ages that homosexual activity is cool and it's something that has no negative or confusing impact on the family and society. Not cool. Very confusing.

The media has been pushing shows that send us the message that it's okay if you're a man and you feel like a woman…just cut your dick off, get a fake vagina, get some big, fake-ass titties sown onto your chest and BAM! YOU ARE NOW A LADY!!! Not.

It's time for somebody to stand up and start talking about the beauty of waiting to have sex until marriage.

It's time for somebody to stand up and start talking about how they did have sexual desires that went against the Bible and God, but they took the time to fight those feelings and not just fall victim to any and every sexual desire and urge that came their way.

It's time for somebody to stand up and start talking about the fact that getting fake titties doesn't make you a female any more than getting a fake dick sewn on your body makes you a man.

Whatever your view is it's important because it's your view. We may not all agree, but what we can agree on is the results. Start looking at the results of certain sexual behavior and see if it's a good thing or a bad thing. Doing this, I believe, will allow the natural design and order of sex to continue to be

a beautiful thing.

It all starts with 1) your view on sex, 2) talking about sex

and 3) making sex education an important topic in church, the

home and schools.

BLACK AND PETTY

When I see a policeman parked in a parking lot trying to be sneaky and catch somebody speeding or setting a speed trap on the highway, I speed up so I'm going at least 10 miles over the speed limit in his face. Why? Because I hate what police officers stand for and how they universally in America have, and continue to have a horrible reputation and track record with black people...and because I'm black and petty.

When I come to a stop sign, I don't do a complete stop. Why? Because I hate what American laws are and how prejudicial they are so if I do a complete stop like I'm supposed to, it means I'm complying with American laws and I don't want to recognize and follow any law system that was geared towards killing and targeting black people...and because I'm black and petty.

When I walk across the street I jay-walk. Why? Once again, America's laws were established to *protect* white people from black people and to give white people whatever edge they could over black people whether it be financial, economic, religious, educational, political or in the area of business and since jaywalking is a law made by white people, I'm not going to adhere to it. That and the fact that I'm black and petty.

I have guns even though I'm technically not supposed to. Why? Since American gun laws allowed white civilian, military and police officers to use their guns to shoot and kill black men without ever seeing a day in jail, I'm not going to abide by *their* unequal gun laws...and I'm black and petty.

When election time rolls around I don't vote. Why? American politics have a horrible history of manipulating voting districts and finding as many ways as possible to not allow black people to participate equally in the voting system.

Also, politicians can declare war and not have their kids go to war. Also, American politics is totally corrupted by big business, racial bias and money so there's not really going to be a difference as to who's in office if everybody has their hands tied by money, the good ole' white boy system and ass-grabbing, so why vote? Also, for the last 400 years, I have a choice to vote between two old ass white men to lead my country as President. That's not really a choice, so that's another big reason why I don't vote. I also don't vote because I'm black and petty.

I don't like going to white churches. Why? White churches and Christianity have tried to teach us that Jesus, all the angels, God and all the prophets were all white guys with blonde hair and blue eyes. Since history, science, the Bible and basic geography show us Jesus and the rest of them *definitely* were not white, I don't go to white churches who still try and push that bullshit rhetoric. I don't like white

Christian songs that sing about, "...wash me and make me whiter than snow..." and other songs that mention the need to be "white and pure like God", so I don't sing any of their songs when I go to a white church. So, for those reasons, I don't like going to white churches. That plus the fact that I'm black and petty.

When I drive down the street and know an old white guy wants to get over in front of me, I used to speed up. Why? I do that because he looks like he is the age of the white men who are responsible for lynching and raping black men, women and children during the period of history before the civil rights movement started. Another reason is because I don't want to give him shit because he probably called grown-ass black men "boy", wouldn't hire a man for being black, loves black female prostitutes and would deny black men bank loans...and because I'm black and petty.

I wrote a Private Matter topic on being black and petty
and put it in this book. Why? Because I wanted to share my
views on American law, religion, politics and other issues from
one black man's perspective...and because sometimes I can be
petty.

INVESTING 101

Why is money so important? It's important because it represents your human value. It represents the amount of time, sweat, blood, tears and creativity a person has invested into our world systems. It represents a person's contribution to society.

When a person has no money, he feels like he has no value. At that point, he or she is willing to sell their body or kill somebody to get money. Sometimes, they are content to simply kill themselves. Life is about value and money gives us that.

The secret is to have some type of gauge to monitor money's value. There needs to be a universal set of laws to achieve this objective. We have seen society's futile and greed-based attempts to manipulate money in favor of certain skin colors or economic class.

As you know, I like to tie everything in life to the Bible...and money is no exception. The book "Claim Your Shit" deals with the ways and reasons to get wealth that are productive. The Bible is full of wealth-building tips and financial advice.

If you want to live a life according to the Bible, your goal is to collect as much wealth as possible so that you can use it to influence the world systems with God's laws and to protect everyone's value. When you are entrusted with wealth, you will know it represents someone's life. It's their life story. It's the measuring stick used to let the world know whether or not he or she provided value to this world system or was a useless piece of shit.

When we let humans decide who should have access to money, and subsequently access to feeling valued or superior, we have all kinds of greed, tax-evasion and corruption. It's when we follow principles for living that are based on a higher-power where we see the best results. Results that are socially beneficial to society.

Jesus was teaching some people a lesson about money and He told them a story about a man who had to leave the country to go get his title as King. He left his servants money based on their ability to invest. When the King returned, he asked the servants how did they do with the money they were entrusted with.

The ones who had the highest financial skills doubled their money; while the one who had the least amount of money did nothing with it. The servants who invested wisely were put in charge of many things by the King. The servant who did nothing with the money was kicked out of the now King's house and thrown into the street for being, as the King said, "wicked, worthless and lazy."

The moral of Jesus' financial lesson? When God entrusts you with wealth and you use it wisely, you will be put in charge of many things. You will be in the continuous position of having wealth at your disposal to invest wisely and control shit. You will be able to control and influence the media, world economies, politics and any other world system.

On the flip-side, if God has blessed you with the skill of investing money and you don't do what you should be doing with it, you will lose your financial position in society and whatever wealth you had.

Lessons like this and other financial lessons Jesus and others in the Bible share with us, are all designed to create Heaven on Earth. When you learn how to claim all the lost dreams and wealth you had access to, you will be put in positions of influence. You will have claimed all the finances you lost that Satan still has control over that he shouldn't, and you will begin to influence your family and society.

I'm glad you read this book. Once you claim all your shit, get ready to start being a person of influence and always remember who it was that died on a cross to legally put you in the position

you are in.

Personal Development Notes

Personal Development Notes

Personal Development Notes

91

Personal Development Notes

Personal Development Notes

Personal Development Notes

www.ingramcontent.com/pod-product-compliance
Lightning Source LLC
Chambersburg PA
CBHW070026260726
48658CB00002B/513